National curriculum

Level 2

activities based on:

'Fox and his friends' & other texts

Kate Grant

Special needs literacy

Contents

	Page
Introduction	3
Week 1 Fox in Trouble (from *Fox and his Friends* by James Marshall)	7
Week 2 Where Next, Mr Noah? (by Mike Dickinson)	13
Week 3 The Boy Who Cried Wolf (by Tony Ross)	19
Week 4 Instructions Make a mask and Make a caterpillar (from Usborne's *What Shall I Make?* by Ray Gibson)	25
Week 5 Humorous poetry 'A for Alice' and 'Don't' (from *Poetry Express 1* and *The Word Party*)	31
Week 6 Information texts Duck (from *See How They Grow* by Angela Royson)	37
Anthology	
Make a mask	43
Make a caterpillar	44
A for Alice	45
Don't	46
Duck	47

Author Kate Grant
Editor Kate Pearce
Assistant editor Roanne Davis
Series designer Paul Cheshire
Designer Paul Roberts
Illustrations Jessica Stockham

Designed using Adobe Pagemaker
Published by Scholastic Ltd, Villiers House, Clarendon Avenue, Leamington Spa, Warwickshire CV32 5PR
Text © Kate Grant
© 2000 Scholastic Ltd
1 2 3 4 5 6 7 8 9 0   0 1 2 3 4 5 6 7 8

British Library Cataloguing-in-Publication Data
A catalogue record for this book is available from the British Library.
ISBN 0-439-01678-9

The right of Kate Grant to be identified as the Author of this Work has been asserted by her in accordance with the Copyright, Designs and Patents Act 1988.

All rights reserved. This book is sold subject to the condition that it shall not, by way of trade or otherwise, be lent, hired out or otherwise circulated without the publisher's prior consent in any form of binding or cover other than that in which it is published and without a similar condition, including this condition, being imposed upon the subsequent purchaser.

No part of this publication may be reproduced, stored in a retrieval system, or transmitted, in any form or by any means, electronic, mechanical, photocopying, recording or otherwise, without the prior permission of the publisher. This book remains copyright, although permission is granted to copy pages marked with the photocopiable icon for classroom distribution and use only in the school which has purchased the book or by the teacher who has purchased the book and in accordance with the CLA licensing agreement. Photocopying permission is given for purchasers only and not for borrowers of books from any lending service.

Acknowledgements

The publishers gratefully acknowledge permission to reproduce the following copyright material:
- **Sheldon Fogelman Agency, Inc.** for the use of text from *Fox and his Friends* by James Marshall © James Marshall (Bodley Head).
- **Scholastic Ltd** for the use of *Where Next, Mr Noah?* By Mike Dickinson © 1997, Mike Dickinson (1997, Little Hippo).
- **Andersen Press** for the use of text from *The Boy Who Cried Wolf* by Tony Ross © 1985, Tony Ross (1985, Andersen Press, London). Also published in paperback by Red Fox and in giant format by Andersen Press.
- **Usborne Publishing** for the use of text and illustrations from *What Shall I Make?* By Ray Gibson © 1995, Ray Gibson (1995, Usborne Publishing, 83–85 Saffron Hill, London EC1N 8RT).
- **Ginn and Company** for the use of 'A for Alice' by June O'Watt from *Poetry Express 1* © June O'Watt (Ginn).
- **Richard Edwards** for the use of 'Don't' by Richard Edwards from *The Word Party* by Richard Edwards © 1986, Richard Edwards (1986, Lutterworth Press).
- **Dorling Kindersley** for the use of text from *Duck* by Angela Royson from the 'See How They Grow' series © Angela Royson (Dorling Kindersley).

Every effort has been made to trace copyright holders for the works reproduced in this book, and the publishers apologize for any inadvertent omissions.

Introduction

Why do I need special needs resources for group time?
The National Literacy Strategy *Framework for Teaching* requires that all children's needs are catered for in the daily Literacy Hour. The class teacher can address individual needs through targeted questions and direct teaching in the first part of the hour when the whole class is taught. However, there is a real necessity for purposeful activities for children with special needs during the group/independent work section of the hour, when the teacher is working elsewhere with guided reading/writing groups. This book is geared to allowing children with special needs to work at an appropriate level on relevant objectives under the guidance of a classroom assistant or other adult.

How does the book work?
Each of the six chapters in this book contains five photocopiable lessons, designed to fit into the 20-minute group/independent work slot in the Literacy Hour and to be used by a classroom assistant or other additional adult. The lessons are based on particular texts, and children working on the activities will need to have access to them. The three story books are:
- *Fox and his Friends* by James Marshall (Red Fox)
- *Where Next, Mr Noah?* by Mike Dickinson (Little Hippo)
- *The Boy Who Cried Wolf* by Tony Ross (Red Fox)

The non-fiction texts and poems are provided as photocopiable pages. One story or extract is the focus for each week's lessons; the activities are at text, sentence and word level and include writing frames and homework tasks.

How does it fit into the Literacy Hour planning?
The genre for the lessons is chosen from the range for Year 3, but the learning objectives are from previous years or terms, since children with special needs are still developing and practising skills from an earlier stage. In this way, if the class is studying legends and fables, for example, the chapter on *The Boy Who Cried Wolf* (Week 3) could be selected for the group working with the classroom assistant.

The objectives are clearly indicated in the grid at the start of each chapter, allowing for simple group target-setting. The same fiction text could be used for guided reading with the group in the previous week if required, although this is not essential.

How flexible is it?
Each chapter in this book can be used independently – there is no need to follow any particular order. Although the texts have been selected to appeal to Year 3 children reading Level 2 texts, they may also be suitable for older children with learning difficulties who are working at this level. The materials can also be used outside the Literacy Hour for additional support if required.

Will classroom assistants need any training to use the book?
Everything that is needed to carry out the group-time lesson is explained in the straightforward notes for each day. There are also useful hints provided in the next few pages to help classroom assistants support children with reading, writing and spelling.

What is the range of the texts?
For Year 3/Level 2, the texts include:
- a story with a familiar setting (*Fox and his Friends*)
- a myth (*Where Next, Mr Noah?*)
- a fable (*The Boy Who Cried Wolf*)

- two instruction texts
- two humorous poems
- an information text.

What objectives are covered?
Learning objectives include:
- **Text level:** characters, playscripts, humour in poems, rhyme and rhythm, alphabetical order, story planning, sequencing in narratives, non-fiction structure, writing instructions, comprehension
- **Sentence level:** exclamation marks, speech marks, questions, verbs
- **Word level:** spelling by analogy, high-frequency words, synonyms, learning new words from reading.

High-frequency words/onset and rime
The following lists show the high frequency words and onset and rime spelling patterns that can be focused on when you are using the texts in the activities.

Fox and his Friends		The Boy Who Cried Wolf		Where Next, Mr Noah?	
down	who	back	little	again	next
said	-ill	people	-old	name	-ain
Instructions		**Humorous poetry**		**Duck**	
take	other	don't	new	this	last
then	-ake	doing	-ock	love	-and

Supported reading
Before choosing a week's lessons, make sure that the text being used is at a suitable reading level (most children in the group should be able to read with no more than one mistake in every ten words).

Fiction books: the lessons which use the story books as their basis assume that the children have already read the books or, in the case of *Fox and his Friends*, one chapter: 'Fox in trouble'. If the children have not already read the book introduce it in the following ways:
- Look at the cover and title – read the title to the children, pointing to the words as you do so.
- Talk together about the author and illustrator, briefly.
- Look through the book together – look at the pictures, discuss what is happening (don't talk about the ending at this stage).

Ask the children to:
- find and read the characters' names in the text
- tell you the story from the pictures
- find key words
- find difficult words and read them aloud together
- explain what some of the tricky words mean

When you read the story, ask them sometimes to read a page as a group, sometimes in turn and sometimes silently. Ask a couple of questions to check that they have understood the story on the pages they have read silently. Check that they are changing the expression in their voices and noticing speech marks and other punctuation.

Non-fiction/information texts: the lessons based on the non-fiction texts do not assume that children will have read the texts before. Although Day 1 for each week explains how to introduce and read the texts, it is helpful to bear in mind the following general points about introducing non-fiction texts:
- Ask the children to read some of the captions to the pictures and the headings for the different sections.
- Help the children to think of some things that the text might help them to learn about.

As with reading fiction, when the children read the text, ask them sometimes to read a section as a group, sometimes in turn, and sometimes silently. Ask a couple of questions to check that they have understood the parts they have read silently.

Poems: the children do not need to have read the two poems before you begin the lessons for Week 5. The notes for Days 1 and 2 explain how to introduce each poem, but you could also help the children to consider how a poem looks different from a story or an information text, and that there is a special term for the author of a poem (poet).

Helping children with reading

Ask the children to tell you how they can work out a word they are finding difficult to read. They could:
- go back to the beginning of the sentence
- say the first sound and think of a word that fits
- leave out the difficult word, read a few more words, then have another try
- look for a little word they know inside the difficult word, for example *l**and**ed*
- look for a pattern they know, for example *old* in *sc**old***

Remind the children of things they should ask themselves as they read:
- Does it make sense?
- Does it sound right?
- Does it look right?

Helping children with writing

The aim should be to enable the children to write as much as possible on their own, and your help will be geared to developing their skills. The writing frames provided in this book give the children a 'scaffold' so that they are not faced with a blank sheet of paper, but you will still need to discuss with them some ideas for what they might want to write. It is a good idea not to let them have pencils until you have finished a preliminary discussion. Have scrap paper or a dry-wipe board and pen available for trying out spellings.

If children ask you how to spell a common (or high-frequency) word that they will need to use fairly often, teach them to spell it by getting them to write it a few times using the Look–Say–Cover–Write–Check method (see page 6).

Another way to help is to draw boxes for the letters in the word (if it is one that can be 'sounded out' fairly easily.) Ask what they can hear at the beginning, middle and end of the word, then help them to put in the missing letters.

For example, if a child wants to write *rocket*, ask him or her to say the word. Once the child can hear the *r*, the *k* in the middle and the *t* at the end, you can help him or her to put the letters in the correct boxes.

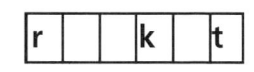

r		k	t

Special Needs Literacy
Resources for Group Time

Next, help the child to say the word again, emphasizing each sound so that he or she can hear more letters. You may need to explain that there is another letter that sounds the same as *k*. The *e* sounds like *i* so you may need to help with this letter, too. Eventually the whole word will appear in the boxes.

| r | o | c | k | e | t |

Encourage the children to keep on reading their sentences as they are writing them, so that they don't leave words out. Remind them to put in capital letters, full stops and so on, and make sure they read their writing through carefully when they have finished.

Supporting spelling (Look–Say–Cover–Write–Check)

If you train children to learn a new word by this method every time they want to remember a spelling, they will nearly always be successful.

> Have a good LOOK at the word.
> SAY the word and spell out the letters.
> COVER the word so that you can't see it.
> WRITE the word down.
> Uncover the word to CHECK if it's right.

The children should repeat the process as often as necessary until they get the word right three times running. Even if the spelling is forgotten later, they will probably have most of the letters right, and relearning will be much quicker the second time.

One reason this method works is because it uses three different ways to learn the same thing. You use your:
- **eyes** to look at the word
- **ears** to hear the letter names as you say them
- **hand** to write the word, and get the feel of its pattern and shape

This gives the brain several chances to store the word in the memory.

It can help children's handwriting development as well as their spelling if they write the words in joined writing, so that they are learning the spelling patterns as a continuous movement.

Making spelling resources

Some of the activities in this book refer to the use of a word wheel and flip book. These can be made very easily and children really do enjoy using them.

Making a word wheel to learn spelling patterns

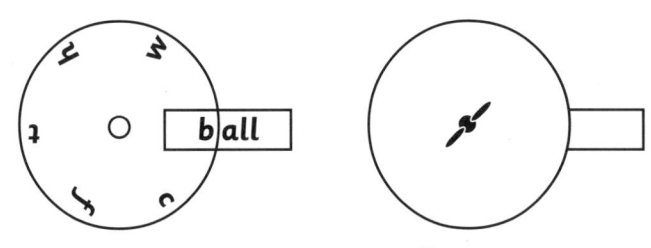

Use a butterfly fastener in the centre of the card.

Reverse

Making a flick book to learn spelling patterns

Staple here.

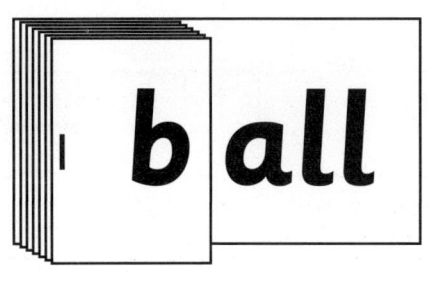

Write a different letter on each small piece of paper to make words, eg *wall, fall, tall* and so on.

Week 1　Fox in Trouble

(from *Fox and his Friends* by James Marshall)

Introduction

The story 'Fox in Trouble' is from the popular series by James Marshall. Books of simple short stories are often seen by children as 'real books' or 'chapter books', which gives them more status in their eyes. Having read and enjoyed one of the stories with support in class, the children can be encouraged to try reading other chapters for themselves.

This story is about Fox, whose mum makes him look after his little sister Louise one Saturday, much against his will. His friends are not able to come out to play, so he takes Louise to the park, where she disappears. He eventually finds her up a telegraph pole, and has to climb up to get her before she will agree to come down. He then bribes her to keep quiet about what has happened.

The story is on two levels. The children should easily understand the obvious 'what happened' level. However, there are also underlying themes of brother–sister relationships and how much of the truth mums should be told! Louise says very little but is obviously a very powerful little girl (or fox). Talking about their own brothers and sisters (and mothers) will help the children to understand the issues in this story.

Week 1 Objectives

	Word level	Sentence level	Text level
Day 1 Reading Discussing characters		To read aloud with intonation and expression Y2 T2 (2) To use awareness of grammar to decipher new words and predict Y2 T2 (1)	To identify and describe characters Y2 T2 (6) To reinforce and apply word level skills Y2 T3 (1)
Day 2 Comprehension Word order		To secure the use of simple sentences Y2 T2 (9) To turn statements into questions Y2 T3 (6)	To make sense of what they have read Y2 T3 (2)
Day 3 Spelling: Sight vocabulary, Onset and rime	To recall high-frequency words Y3 T1–3 (3) Spelling by analogy with known words Y3 T1–3 (6)		
Day 4 Speech marks Synonyms	To collect, discuss and use synonyms Y2 T3 (10)	To identify speech marks in reading Y2 T2 (6)	
Day 5 Writing composition			To write simple playscripts based on own reading Y3 T1 (15) To apply phonological and graphic knowledge and sight vocabulary to spell words Y2 T3 (9)
Homework task 1 Cloze		To predict from the text, read on, leave a gap and re-read Y2 T2 (1)	To make sense of what they have read Y2 T3 (2)
Homework task 2 Wordsearch	To read on sight and spell high-frequency words Y2 T2 (6)		

Reading

The children should have already read this chapter with the teacher in supported reading (see page 4).

With the children

Quickly look through the book with the children, just to remind them of the story. Ask the children to talk in pairs for a minute or two, then see if they can give the main point of the story in just two or three sentences.

Read a page to the children, without any expression and without varying your voice to sound like different characters. Ask the children what is wrong. Now ask them each to read a page, noticing speech marks and changing the intonation in their voices.

After reading

Discussing characters

- Who are the main characters in this story? (Fox and Louise)
- Are there any other characters in the story? (Mum, Betty, Dexter and their mums)
- What sort of character is Fox? Do you like him or not?
- Do you think he likes Louise? Does he want to play with her?
- Why does he buy her an ice cream?
- Do you think it is right to bribe someone to do something?

Special Needs Literacy

Comprehension

Quiz (oral answers)

1. Who is older, Louise or Fox?
A. Fox.
2. Why couldn't Dexter go out to play?
A. He had to help at home.
3. Which word lets us know that Fox was worried when he couldn't find Louise?
A. 'serious'.
4. What was wrong with Betty?
A. She had chicken pox.
5. Why did Fox buy Louise an ice cream?
A. So that she wouldn't tell Mum what had happened.

Quiz (written answers)

1. What day was it in the story?
A. Saturday.
2. What did Betty say to Fox?
A. "Sorry, Fox".
3. What did Louise say when Fox told her to come down?
A. "Come and get me"; "No!".
4. Who do you think is most clever, Louise or Fox?
A. Personal opinion (probably Louise).
5. Do you think Louise should have told her mum what really happened?
A. Personal opinion.

Word order

- Write the following sentence (from page 5) on a strip of card and cut the strip into separate words. Write the full stop on its own card.

  But today you must take care of little Louise.

- Help the children to rearrange the words into a different order, to make other sentences. For example:

  But must you take care of little Louise today?

- How is this sentence different? (It's a question.) Do you need a full stop? (No, a question mark.)
- How many sentences can the children make? For example:

  But you must take care of little Louise today.

- Can you leave any words out and still have a sensible sentence?

  You must take care of Louise.

- Can you change the meaning completely?

  But today little Louise must take care of you.

- What is the shortest sentence you can make? For instance:

  Take care of Louise.

Special Needs Literacy

Sight vocabulary

Ask the children to find the word *down* (page 16) and to learn to spell the word using the Look–Say–Cover–Write–Check–method (see page 6) until they can write it from memory. Do the same with *little* (page 5) and *said*. The children should write the words in their spelling books to take home for further practice.

Help the children to think of a sentence with all three words in it and to write it down, using a coloured pen to highlight *down*, *said* and *little*.

Spelling by analogy

Spelling pattern: -ill
Ask the children to find *will* (page 21) and to look carefully at the word. They should learn to spell the word using the Look–Say–Cover–Write–Check method (see page 6) until they can write it from memory.

Encourage them to think of words that rhyme with *will* (*hill, pill, fill, still, grill, Jill*). Dictate the words for the children to write in their spelling books.

Dictate the following sentences, for the children to write down. (Decide whether you want them to have the word list for reference or not.) Remind them about capital letters and full stops, if necessary.

Jill is **ill**, so she **will** take a **pill**.
Fill the cup, take it up the **hill**, but don't **spill** it.

The children should underline all the *-ill* words in their completed sentences with a coloured pencil or felt-tipped pen.

They could make word wheels or flick books with the spelling pattern to take home (see page 6).

Week 1 Fox in Trouble — Day 3

Speech marks

- Ask the children to find all the speech marks on pages 8 and 9. Who is speaking each time?
- Ask four children to take the parts of Betty, Fox, Louise and Betty's mum, and to read just the dialogue, making it sound like 'real talking'.
- Ask the children to write down this sentence and then complete it. They can write the speech marks in a different colour.

"No," said Fox. "I don't…

Synonyms

- Ask the children to find the word *awful* (page 10) and to read the sentence in which it appears.
- Turn to page 20. Which word means the same as *awful*? (*terrible*)
- Help the children to think of other words that mean the same (or nearly the same) as *awful* and *terrible* (for instance, *difficult, annoying, upsetting, dreadful, horrible*).
- Test each word by substituting it for *awful* and *terrible* in the sentences in the story.
- Help the children to think of and write a sentence using one of the new words. You could tell them that 'synonym' is the correct term for 'words that mean the same thing'.

Week 1 Fox in Trouble — Day 4

Fox in trouble again

Scene: The next day in Fox's house.

Fox: Mum, can I go out on my bike, please?

Mum: No, Fox. I told you this morning that I want you to take Louise to the library to get a new story book.

Fox: Oh, Mum, you're joking.

Mum:

Fox:

Louise:

———

———

———

———

———

Writing composition:
Tell the children that they are going to write a story about Fox, but this time it is going to be a playscript with just the words that each character speaks.

Fox in trouble

Read the story and put the missing words (at the bottom of the page) back in the right places.

One _____, Fox had to look after little sister, Louise.

None of his _____ could come out to play, so he took

Louise to the _____. "This is awful!" he _____.

Fox did not want to look _____ Louise. When he

looked around, Louise wasn't there. She had _____ up

a telegraph pole and would not come _____ until Fox

climbed up to get her.

Fox hated _____ places but he had to do it. Fox

was _____ that Louise would _____ mum

so he got her a _____ big ice cream to keep her

_____.

park	climbed	friends	worried
Saturday	down	high	said
very	after	tell	quiet

Fox in Trouble

Wordsearch

Find each of these words in the wordsearch square. Colour in each word as you find it.

serious	Saturday	Louise	fox
fun	home	park	mum
down	still	all	she

f	o	x	s	o	r	r	y
n	m	u	m	h	o	m	e
s	t	i	l	l	s	h	e
n	o	L	o	u	i	s	e
S	a	t	u	r	d	a	y
t	f	u	n	a	l	l	h
s	e	r	i	o	u	s	k
p	a	r	k	d	o	w	n

Can you find five more words? Some words may be hidden inside others.

1
2
3
4
5

Week 2　Where Next, Mr Noah?

by Mike Dickinson

Introduction

This book, from the *Read with Little Hippo* series is an ideal text for children who are at the stage where they are moving away from dependence on the familiar structure of reading schemes to reading individual stories. There is a small amount of text on each page along with supporting illustrations, and the storyline is carried along by a repetitive theme. Mr and Mrs Noah and all the animals have been cooped up in the ark for weeks. Now, at last, the rain has stopped and the floodwater has gone, but Mr Noah has a lot of work to do, deciding where to send the animals and trying to persuade them that he knows best. Not all the animals are easy to please.

(As *Where Next, Mr Noah?* does not have page numbers you may find it helpful to number the pages using small sticky labels for finding specific pages during the activities. Begin the numbering from the title page.)

Week 2 Objectives

	Word level	Sentence level	Text level
Day 1 Reading Discussing characters	To learn new words from reading Y2 T1 (10)	To read aloud with intonation and expression Y2 T2 (2) To use awareness of grammar to decipher new words and predict Y2 T2 (1)	To reinforce and apply word level skills Y2 T3 (1) To identify and describe characters Y2 T2 (6)
Day 2 Retelling the story Comprehension			To make sense of what they have read Y2 T3 (2)
Day 3 Spelling: Sight vocabulary, Onset and rime	To recall high-frequency words Y3 T1–3 (3) Spelling by analogy with known words Y3 T1–3 (6)		
Day 4 Synonyms Speech marks	To use synonyms and other alternative words and phrases Y2 T3 (10)	To identify speech marks in reading Y2 T2 (6)	
Day 5 Writing composition			To plan main points as a structure for story writing Y3 T2 (6)
Homework Task 1 Word order		To re-order sentences Y1 T3 (4)	
Homework Task 2 Comprehension			To make sense of what they have read Y2 T3 (2)

Day 1 — Week 2 Where Next, Mr Noah?

Reading

The children should have already read this book with the teacher in supported reading (see page 4).

Look through the book quickly with the children, just to remind them of the story. Ask the children to talk in pairs for a minute or two, and see if they can tell the main point of the story in just two or three sentences.

Ask each child to choose their favourite part of the story and read those pages to the group.

After reading
Discussing characters

- Who are the main characters in this story? (Mr and Mrs Noah)
- What kind of a character is Mr Noah? Can the children find parts of the story which show this?
- Does he ever get fed up? How do you know?
- Which animal characters are lazy? (Condors) How do you know?
- Which animal characters are playful? (Boa constrictors) How do you know?
- Which animal characters are fussy? (Camels) How do you know?

Special Needs Literacy

Day 2 — Week 2 Where Next, Mr Noah?

Retelling

Ask the children to retell the story taking turns to say a sentence, and trying to link it to the previous one using connectives such as *next, but, then, after that, finally*. Encourage them to use their own words and to produce a sentence which covers a few pages of the story, rather than just one.

Comprehension

Quiz (oral answers)
1. Who is the story about?
A. Mr and Mrs Noah and the animals.
2. Where does the story come from?
A. The bible.
3. Why did Mr Noah send the kangaroos to Australia?
A. So they had room to jump.
4. How did Mr Noah trick the condors?
A. He sent them far away (to South America).
5. Where did Mr Noah send the elephants?
A. Africa and India

Quiz (written answers)
1. What do kangaroos like to do?
A. Jump.
2. Do African elephants have big or little ears?
A. Big.
3. Who eats bamboo shoots?
A. Pandas.
4. Fill in the missing word. Mr Noah said the condors were lazy _____.
A. birds.
5. Mr Noah looked in an atlas. True or false?
A. True.

Special Needs Literacy

Special Needs Literacy
Resources for Group Time

Sight vocabulary

Ask the children to find the word *back* (page 8) and to learn to spell the word using the Look–Say–Cover–Write–Check method (see page 6) until they can write it from memory. Do the same with *next* (page 11) and *name* (page 10). The children should write the words in their spelling books to take home for further practice.

Help the children to think of a sentence with all three words in it, and to write it down, using a coloured pencil or felt-tipped pen to highlight *back*, *next* and *name*.

Spelling by analogy

Spelling pattern: *-ain*

Ask the children to find *rain* (page 3) and to look carefully at the word. They should learn to spell the word using the Look–Say–Cover–Write–Check method (see page 6) until they can write it from memory.

Encourage them to think of words that rhyme with rain (*Spain, train, pain, chain, drain*). Dictate the words for the children to write in their spelling books.

Dictate the following sentences, for the children to write down. (Decide whether you want them to have the word list for reference or not.) Remind them about capital letters and full stops, if necessary.

*I went to **Spain** on a **train** in the **rain**.
My **chain** fell down the **drain**.*

The children should underline all the *-ain* words in their completed sentences with a coloured pencil or felt-tipped pen.

They could make word wheels or flick books with the spelling pattern to take home (see page 6).

Day 3 — Week 2 Where Next, Mr Noah?

Synonyms

Ask the children to find words in the first few pages that tell you how a character said something (*yelled, called, shouted, asked*). Remind them that these words are called *verbs*. Help the children to think of other verbs to use instead of *said*. (For example, Mrs Noah *cried* and *gasped* after the animals had gone.)

Ask the children to write some sentences of their own, each containing one of the verbs from the book. They can then find and colour the verbs in their sentences.

Speech marks

Ask the children to find the speech marks. (Point them out if they are having difficulty). Remind them that these are 'talking marks' and show the actual words someone said.

In turn, ask each child to choose a page with speech marks and practise reading it with as much expression as possible.

Ask the children to write this sentence down and then complete it. They can write the speech marks in a different colour.

"Mr Noah," said the cat, "Can I...?"

Day 4 — Week 2 Where Next, Mr Noah?

The next adventure of the _____

The _____ left the Ark, with their packed lunches, on their way to _____.

First

Then

Next

Finally

Writing composition:
Ask the children to write a story about what happened next to one of the animals in *Where Next, Mr Noah?* using the writing frame above.

Where Next, Mr Noah?

Sentence jumble

The words in these sentences from *Where Next, Mr Noah?* have become mixed up. Can you write each one correctly? Look for the capital letter to help you start.

1 day stopped the One the and rain out. came sun

_____

_____

2 are for Bamboo good shoots tummies. wobbly

_____

_____

3 swept and under the Mr looked the all floors Noah beds.

_____

_____

4 went Mrs to Noah make inside tea. of cup a

_____

_____

Where Next, Mr Noah?

Quiz

See if you can you remember what happened in *Where Next, Mr Noah?* by answering these questions.

1 Do African elephants have big ears or little ears?

_____

2 Which animal eats bamboo shoots?

_____

3 Who went to Australia?

_____

4 What did the boa constrictors want to do?

_____

5 Who wanted to go with the dogs?

_____

Week 3 The Boy Who Cried Wolf
by Tony Ross

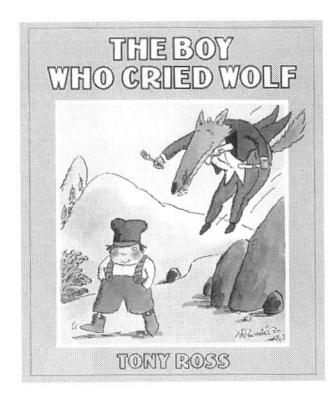

Introduction

This famous story of the boy who cried 'Wolf' may well be one the children already know. Tony Ross, a deservedly popular children's author, retells the 'cautionary tale' with wit and humour. His illustrations are very amusing and support the text well, which makes it easier for children to predict unfamiliar words as they read. It is a book that lends itself particularly well to being read aloud, and to making the most of exclamation marks! Harry enjoyed tricking everyone into thinking the wolf was coming, until the day he really needed them to believe him, but no one did. The wolf's lack of scruples as he eats not only the naughty Harry but the grown-ups as well, is designed to appeal to children.

(As *The Boy Who Cried Wolf* does not have page numbers you may find it helpful to number the pages using small sticky labels for finding specific pages during the activities. Begin the numbering from the title page.)

Week 3 Objectives

	Word level	Sentence level	Text level
Day 1 Reading Discussion	To learn new words from reading Y2 T1 (10)	To read aloud with intonation and expression Y2 T2 (2) To use awareness of grammar to decipher new words and predict Y2 T2 (1)	To reinforce and apply word level skills Y2 T3 (1)
Day 2 Comprehension Exclamation marks		To recognise and take account of exclamation marks in reading Y2 T1 (3)	To make sense of what they have read Y2 T3 (2)
Day 3 Spelling: Sight vocabulary, Onset and rime	To recall high-frequency words Y3 T1–3 (3) Spelling by analogy with known words Y3 T1–3 (6)		
Day 4 Making questions from statements Syllables	To discriminate syllables in multisyllabic words Y2 T2 (5)	To turn statements into questions Y2 T3 (6)	
Day 5 Writing composition			To write a story plan for own fable Y3 T2 (9) To apply phonological and graphic knowledge and sight vocabulary to spell words Y2 T3 (9)
Homework task 1 Sentence order			To make sense of what they read Y2 T3 (2)
Homework task 2 Book review			To write simple evaluations of books read Y2 T3 (12)

Week 3 — The Boy Who Cried Wolf

Day 1

Reading

The children should have already read this book with the teacher in supported reading (see page 4).

With the children

Can the children remember what a *fable* is? (A story with an important message.) Look through the book quickly with the children to remind them of the story. Ask them to talk in pairs for a minute or two, then see if they can give a summary of the story in just two or three sentences.

What is the important message of the story? (Don't tell lies, or nobody will believe you when you do tell the truth.)

Ask the children to find *lap of luxury* (page 4). Can they remember what it means? Discuss why "WOLF!" (pages 16–19) is in capital letters. Ask the children to practise reading pages 16–19 with appropriate expression.

The comment at the end of the book, in French – *C'est la vie* (That's life) – may need explaining.

After reading

Discussion

- Did Harry deserve what happened to him?
- Did the adults deserve to be eaten?
- Is lying always wrong?

Special Needs Literacy

Day 2

Comprehension

Quiz (oral answers)

1. Where did Harry live?
A. On this side of the mountains.
2. What was the wolf's name?
A. We don't know.
3. Name two things Harry hated doing.
A. Having baths; going to violin lessons.
4. Why didn't his grandmother believe him?
A. He was always crying "Wolf!"
5. When did the wolf change his mind about eating Harry?
A. When he saw the grown-ups.

Quiz (written answers)

1. What was the boy's name in the story?
A. Harry.
2. True or False? Harry was on roller-skates when he saw the wolf.
A. False.
3. What did Harry cry in his violin lesson?
A. "Wolf!"
4. Do you think the wolf was greedy?
A. Personal opinion.
5. Fill in the missing words "You shouldn't have _____ so many _____."
A. told, lies.

Exclamation marks

- Find examples in the book of *"Wolf!"* (followed by an exclamation mark) and *wolf* in the middle of a sentence (for example: *The wolf had fine manners*).
- Help the children to hear the difference the exclamation mark makes when they are reading. Find examples, in the book, of sentences which end with an exclamation mark. For example:

"Tell me another one!" (page 17)
"Save me from the WOLF!" (page 19)
"You shouldn't have told so many lies!" (page 20)

- Is there a full stop as well? No – an exclamation mark is used instead of a full stop.
- Practise reading these sentences with as much expression as possible. Then read them again as if there were no exclamation marks. Can the children hear the difference?
- Think of other expressions where an exclamation mark could be used (for instance, *Help! Stop!*).
- Ask the children to write two sentences of their own which end in exclamation marks.

Special Needs Literacy

Sight vocabulary

Ask the children to find *who* (in the title) and to learn to spell the word using the Look–Say–Cover–Write–Check method (see page 6) until they can write it from memory. Do the same with *again* (last page) and *people* (page 7). The children should write the words in their spelling books to take home for further practice.

Help the children to think of a sentence with all three words in it, and to write it down, using a coloured pencil or felt-tipped pen to highlight *who*, *again* and *people*.

Spelling by analogy

Spelling pattern: -old

Ask the children to find *told* (page 20) and to look carefully at the word. They should learn to spell the word using the Look–Say–Cover–Write–Check method (see page 6) until they can write it from memory.

Encourage them to think of words that rhyme with *told* (*sold, cold, hold, fold, bold, gold*). Dictate the words for the children to write in their spelling books.

Dictate the following sentences, for the children to write in their spelling books. (Decide whether you want them to have the word list for reference or not.) Remind them about capital letters and full stops, if necessary.

*I **told** you to **hold** on to the **gold**
Tom **told** me he **sold** his **old** toys.*

The children should underline all the *-old* words in their completed sentences with a coloured pencil or felt-tipped pen.

They could make word wheels or flick books with the spelling pattern to take home (see page 6).

Week 3 The Boy Who Cried Wolf — Day 3

Special Needs Literacy

Making questions from statements

- Write this sentence on a strip of card for the children to read:

    Everybody was afraid of the wolf.

- Can the children turn the sentence into a question?

    Was everybody afraid of the wolf?

- What do you need to change? (The order of the words and the position of the capital letter. The full stop also needs to become a question mark.)

- Can you always use exactly the same words when you change a statement into a question? For example, to turn this statement:

    The wolf liked to eat people.

    into this question:

    Did the wolf like to eat people?

    what do you need to change?
    (*Liked* to *like* and add the word *did*.)

- Can the children turn this statement into other questions, for example:

    Why did the wolf like to eat people?

- Help the children to find other statements from the story and turn them into questions.

Syllables

- Ask the children to find the word *mountains* (page 3)
- Clap the syllables in the word (two claps: *mount/ains*).
- Ask the children to read page 3 again to find another word that has two syllables (*little, upon, Harry*).
- Help the children to count the syllables in these words by clapping as they say them.

wolf   (1)
Harry   (2)
whenever   (3) page 8
name   (1) page 3
believe   (2) page 17
everybody   (4) page 7
grandmother (3) page 17

- Each child in turn chooses a page and claps the syllables in a word, without saying it aloud. The others have to guess what the word was.
- Ask the children to choose words of one, two, three and four syllables from the story. They should then write down each word, highlighting each syllable in a different colour.

Week 3 The Boy Who Cried Wolf — Day 4

Special Needs Literacy

Special Needs Literacy
Resources for Group Time

The _____ who cried "Wolf!"

Setting: Where does the story happen?

Main characters: What are their names? What are they like?

Beginning: How does the story start?

Two things that happen in my story:

1

2

Ending:

Writing composition:
Help the children to make a plan of their own story about a boy or girl who cried "Wolf!" using this writing frame.

Story jumble

These sentences from *The Boy Who Cried Wolf* have become mixed up. Put a number beside each one to show the correct order.

○ One day the wolf really did jump out and Harry ran back to town crying, "WOLF!"

○ The grown-ups said sternly, "You shouldn't have told so many lies!"

○ Harry used to cry, "Wolf!" just for fun.

○ Nobody believed Harry this time.

○ The wolf ate the grown-ups. Then he had Harry for supper.

○ A little boy called Harry lived on this side of the mountains.

The Boy Who Cried Wolf

Book review

I have just read

written by

illustrated by

published by

I thought that the book was

because

The part I liked best was

I didn't like

I would recommend this book to

I would give it a score of

Boring										Brilliant
0	1	2	3	4	5	6	7	8	9	10

Reviewed by

Week 4 Instructions

('Make a mask' and 'Make a caterpillar' from Usborne's *What Shall I Make?* by Ray Gibson)

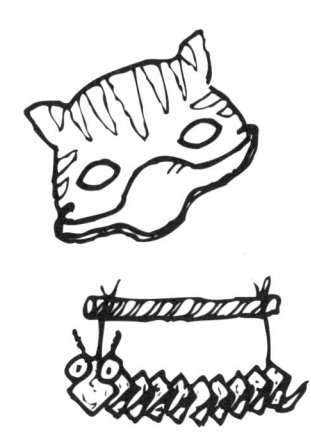

Introduction

The two extracts focused on in this chapter provide instructions for how to make simple masks and dancing caterpillars. Although the instructions are easy to follow, it would be too time-consuming to make a mask or caterpillar during the Literacy Hour. However, if they wanted to, the children could take the photocopiable sheets home in order to try making them.

Reading and understanding non-fiction is an important skill for children to develop. Information texts look different from stories, and even very simple texts such as these contain more formal, precise language, and require a different approach. Writing their own instructions (see Day 5 and Homework Task 1) will encourage children to begin to use the appropriate structures and features of information texts.

Week 4 Objectives

	Word level	Sentence level	Text level
Day 1 Reading Comprehension	To learn new words from reading Y2 T1 (10)	To read aloud with intonation and expression Y2 T2 (2) To use awareness of grammar to decipher new words and predict Y2 T2 (1)	To reinforce and apply word level skills Y2 T3 (1) To note key structural features of non-fiction texts Y2 T1 (14)
Day 2 Sequencing Comprehension			To make sense of what they have read Y2 T3 (2)
Day 3 Spelling Sight vocabulary Onset and rime	To recall high-frequency words Y3 T1–3 (3) Spelling by analogy with known words Y3 T1–3 (6)		
Day 4 Verbs Alphabetical ordering		To use verb tenses with increasing accuracy Y2 T2 (5)	To use alphabetically ordered texts Y2 T2 (18)
Day 5 Writing composition			To use models from reading to order instructions sequentially Y2 T1 (16) To write simple instructions Y2 T1 (15)
Homework task 1 Writing instructions			To write simple instructions Y2 T1 (15)
Homework task 2 Wordsearch	To read on sight and spell high-frequency words Y2 T2 (6)		

Reading

Before reading

Look at the 'Make a mask' extract on page 43 with the children and ask them what they think it is about. Is it a story? How do they know it isn't? What do they expect to find out about? While you are talking, use the word 'instructions'. Make sure the children understand the term.

Look through the extract with the children, paying attention to the layout and the use of pictures. Explain to the children that this is a non-fiction text. Ask them what is the difference between fiction and non-fiction. (Fiction refers to stories and is not necessarily true; non-fiction is about facts and things which really happen or things you can do.) This kind of non-fiction text is called instructional.

Help the children to think of other examples of instructions (such as recipes, how to play a game, school rule lists). Talk about the way the information is organized. Introduce the terms 'captions' and 'layout'.

Read the text together.

After reading

Make a word web together, showing all the materials and so on which are needed to make a mask (see the diagram below).

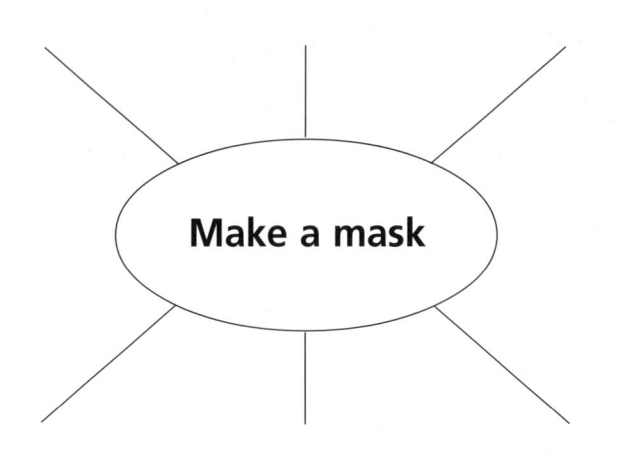

Make a mask

Week 4 Instructions — Day 1

Special Needs Literacy

Sequencing

Let the children briefly look at the instructions for 'Make a caterpillar'. In turn, without looking at the text if possible, the children repeat the instructions in their own words, trying to keep them in the correct order. Encourage the children to use words like *first, next, then, after that, finally*.

Comprehension

Quiz (oral or written answers)

1. What is the last thing you do to make a caterpillar?
A. Tie it onto a straw.
2. Name three things you need to make a caterpillar.
A. Choose from: bright paper, sponge, paints, glue, material for the eyes, feelers and tail, thin elastic, a straw.
3. What do you put on the caterpillar's head?
A. Eyes and feelers.
4. Why do you use elastic and not string?
A. So that the caterpillar will jump around.
5. Instructions show you how to _____ something.
A. make.

Week 4 Instructions — Day 2

Special Needs Literacy

Special Needs Literacy
Resources for Group Time

Sight vocabulary

Ask the children to find the word *put* in 'Make a mask' and to learn to spell the word using the Look–Say–Cover–Write–Check method (see page 6) until they can write it from memory. Do the same with *then* and *other*. The children should write the words in their spelling books to take home for further practice.

Help the children to think of a sentence with all three words in it, and to write it down, using a coloured pencil or felt-tipped pen to highlight *put, then* and *other*.

Spelling by analogy

Spelling pattern: *-ake*

Ask the children to find the word *take* and look carefully at the spelling. They should learn to spell the word using the Look–Say–Cover–Write–Check method (see page 6) until they can write it from memory.

Encourage them to think of words that rhyme with *take (make, cake, bake, shake, lake, snake)*. Dictate the words for the children to write in their spelling books

Dictate the following sentences, for the children to write in their spelling books. (Decide whether you want them to have the word list for reference or not.) Remind them about capital letters and full stops, if necessary.

*Can a **snake bake** a **cake**?*
*Don't **shake** the **rake** at me.*

Ask the children to underline all the *-ake* words in their completed sentences with a coloured pencil or felt-tipped pen.

They could make word wheels or flick books with the spelling pattern to take home (see page 6).

Day 3 — Week 4 Instructions

Verbs

Ask the children if they know what kind of a word a verb is. Make sure that they understand it is an 'action word' or a word for something that can be done.

Ask the children to find all the verbs in the 'Make a mask' section, which tell them what you have to do to make a mask (*take, fold, put, draw, add, poke, push, cut, glue, turn, paint, tie*). They can highlight the words in colour.

Past tense

- Tell the children to imagine they have already made a mask and are telling the rest of the class how they did it, using the same verbs as above. For example:

    draw: I **drew** around the shape.
    cut: I **cut** out the eyeholes.
    fold: I **folded** the paper.
    paint: I **painted** the mask.

- Write down the verbs and their past tenses and ask the children what they notice. For instance, some words have an 'ed' ending and others don't.
- Help the children to write their own sentences using verbs in the past tense. They can colour the verbs.

Alphabetical ordering

- Read the verbs on the list you made (opposite) with the children. Practise reciting the alphabet with them if they do not already know it.
- Help the children to put the verbs in alphabetical order in a list. Three verbs begin with 'p' so you will need to discuss using the second letter of these words to find their alphabetical order.

    cut
    draw
    fold
    glue
    paint
    poke
    put
    turn

- If you have time, do the same thing with the words from the word web for the items needed to make a mask from Day 1.

Day 4 — Week 4 Instructions

How to make a _____

First

Then

Next

Finally

Writing composition:
Ask the children to think of something they know how to make, such as a sandwich or a milkshake. Then ask them to write instructions to tell other children how to make it using the writing frame above. They could draw pictures, too.

Instructions

Writing instructions

Think of something that you know how to make, like a paper aeroplane or a fan. (If you can't think of anything, ask someone to show you how to make something first.) Now write careful instructions to tell other children how to make it themselves.

How to make _____

You will need

First

Then

Next

Finally

Wordsearch

Find each of these words in the wordsearch square. Colour in each word as you find it.

elastic	glue	mask	corner	scissors
turn	cut	draw	shape	edge	holes

h	o	l	e	s	c	u	t
s	s	h	a	p	e	o	n
t	u	r	n	m	a	s	k
s	c	i	s	s	o	r	s
d	r	a	w	w	a	s	j
e	d	g	e	g	l	u	e
t	o	c	o	r	n	e	r
e	l	a	s	t	i	c	t

Can you find five more words? Some words may be hidden inside others.

1

2

3

4

5

Week 5 Humorous poetry

('A for Alice' by June O'Watt and 'Don't' by Richard Edwards from *Poetry Express 1* and *The Word Party*)

Introduction

These two amusing poems chosen for Week 5 are easily accessible and follow formats which are easy to understand. 'A for Alice' is a 'pattern' poem, following the letters of the alphabet. It provides an opportunity to revise alphabetical order in an interesting context. It is easy for children to use as a model for their own writing and they can personalize their own versions by using the names of friends. 'Don't' is a humorous poem about the naughty or silly things children are told not to do by grown-ups. Both poems have an obvious rhyme pattern and a strong rhythm which makes them very satisfying to learn and recite.

Week 5 Objectives

	Word level	Sentence level	Text level
Day 1 Reading poetry	To learn new words from reading Y2 T1 (10)	To read aloud with intonation and expression Y2 T2 (2) To use awareness of grammar to decipher new words and predict Y2 T2 (1)	To read and respond imaginatively to humorous poems Y2 T3 (6) To identify and discuss patterns of rhythm and rhyme Y2 T2 (9)
Day 2 Comprehension			To make sense of what they have read Y2 T3 (2) To discuss words that create humour Y2 T3 (8)
Day 3 Spelling: Sight vocabulary, Onset and rime	To recall high-frequency words Y3 T1–3 (3) Spelling by analogy with known words Y3 T1–3 (6)		
Day 4 Verbs Alphabetical order		To understand the function of verbs in sentences Y3 T1 (3) To understand the need for grammatical agreement Y2 T3 (2)	To use alphabetically ordered texts Y2 T2 (18) To comment on the impact of layout Y3 T1 (7)
Day 5 Writing composition			To use structures from poems as a basis for writing Y2 T2 (15)
Homework task 1 Cloze		To predict from the text, read on, leave a gap and re-read Y2 T2 (1)	To make sense of what they have read Y2 T3 (2)
Homework task 2 Alphabetical order			To use alphabetically ordered texts Y2 T2 (18)

Day 1 — Week 5 Humorous poetry

Reading
Give each child a copy of 'A for Alice' (page 45).
- Ask the children how the poem is organized (alphabetical order).
- Practise reciting the alphabet, first as a group, then with each child saying four letters in turn.
- Read the poem, with each child reading two lines in turn.
- Now read the poem again, as a group.
- Talk about the way the text is organized. How is it different from a story? Point out that the layout is in lines, not sentences that follow on.
- Read the first four lines of 'A for Alice'. Can the children hear any rhymes?
- Make sure they notice that the rhymes are in pairs, and at the ends of the lines. You could tell them that the name for this sort of rhyming pattern is 'rhyming couplets'.
- Help them to think of other words that rhyme with the words in the poem, and to make up alternative lines. For example:

A for Alice who climbed a tree
B for Brad who hurt his knee

- In pairs, the children choose a letter, recite the line from the poem for their letter, then make up a different rhyming line for the following letter.

Comprehension
Quiz (oral answers)
1. Who was awfully sick?
A. Dennis.
2. Whose name begins with T?
A. Tracey.
3. Where did Paul sit down?
A. In a puddle.
4. What can Gemma make?
A. Bread.
5. Who is a good runner?
A. Shazeia.

Special Needs Literacy

Day 2 — Week 5 Humorous poetry

Reading
Give each child a copy of 'Don't' (page 46).
- Ask the children to look at the poem. Do they notice what is the same about each line? (They all begin with *Don't*.)
- Ask the children what sort of things they do that adults say 'Don't' to.
- Read the poem to the children first, while they follow the text.
- Now read the poem again, this time as a group.
- Ask each child in turn which line they find the most amusing.
- What makes this poem funny?
- Look at the rhyme pattern and compare it to 'A for Alice'. How is the rhyme pattern in this poem different? (The rhyme is at the end of every other line.)
- Help the children to highlight pairs of rhyming words on their copies of the poem.
- Do rhyming words always have to have the same spelling pattern? Ask the children to find some words that do (*cat/that, chair/hair*) and some that don't (*do/new, tea/me*).

Comprehension
Quiz (written answers)
1. What should you not do to the cat?
A. Kiss it.
2. What rhymes with *clocks* in the poem?
A. Socks.
3. What should you not feed?
A. The chair.
4. What should you not wash?
A. Books.
5. What rhymes with *chair* in the poem?
A. Hair.

Special Needs Literacy
Resources for Group Time

An alphabet poem ABC

A for Adam who

B for

—

D

—

F

—

—

I

—

—

—

M

—

Writing composition:
Ask the children to write their own alphabet poem using the writing frame above. Tell them to put in all the letters of the alphabet as far as N, first. Encourage them to try to use different names from the ones in 'A for Alice'. Are they going to include themselves and their friends? They could complete the poem, on the back of the sheet, outside the Literacy Hour.

Sight vocabulary

Ask the children to find the word *don't* and to look carefully at the spelling. They should learn to spell the word using the Look–Say–Cover–Write–Check method (see page 6) until they can write it from memory.

Do the same with *new* and *doing*. The children should write the words in their spelling books to take home for further practice.

Help the children to think of a sentence with all three words in it, and to write it down, using a coloured pencil or felt-tipped pen to highlight *don't*, *new* and *doing*.

Spelling by analogy

Ask the children to find *socks* and *clocks* and to look carefully at the spelling. They should learn to spell *sock* using the Look–Say–Cover–Write–Check method (see page 6) until they can write it from memory.

Encourage them to think of words that rhyme with *sock* and *clock* (*shock, lock, rock, tock*).

Dictate the words for the children to write in their spelling books. Now dictate the following sentences, for the children to write in their spelling books. (Decide whether you want them to have the word list for reference or not.) Remind them about capital letters and full stops, if necessary.

*What a **shock**, a **rock** is in my **sock**.*
*The **clock** went tick **tock**.*

The children should underline all the -*ock* words in their completed sentences with a coloured pencil or felt-tipped pen.

They could make word wheels or flick books with the spelling pattern to take home (see page 6).

Special Needs Literacy

Verbs

Ask the children if they know what kind of a word a verb is. Make sure they understand that it is an 'action word' or a word for something that can be done.
- Ask the children to find all the verbs, in the poem, for example *slurp*, *bubble*.
- They can circle the verbs in colour on their own copies of the poem.
- Ask how they could respond to each *Don't…* line in the poem? For example:

Don't **slurp** your spaghetti
I'm not **slurping** my spaghetti
Don't **kiss** the cat
I'm not **kissing** the cat.

- Help the children to notice what has happened to the verb (-*ing* has been added).
- The children can choose a few lines of the poem and write their own answers, underlining the verbs in all the lines.

Special Needs Literacy

Humorous poetry

Don't

Read the poem and put the missing words (at the bottom of the page) back in the right places.

Don't _____ your spaghetti

Don't kiss the _____

Don't butter _____ fingers

Don't walk like that

Don't draw on the _____

Don't _____ all the clocks

Don't water the _____

_____ hide _____ socks

Oh, _____ do people say "don't" so much,

When ever you try _____ new?

It's more _____ doing the don'ting

So why don't people say _____?

"do"	fun	change	cat
slurp	your	pillow	phone
why	Don't	something	my

Humorous poetry

Alphabet mess

These names should be in alphabetical order, but they are mixed up. Can you write a new list, in alphabetical order?

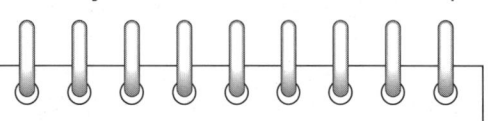

Wendy
Carol
Alice
Ian
Yael
Leon
Paul
Hannah
Kate
Nick
Oliver
Tracy
Xavier
Ernest
George
Ben
Maria
Victor
David
Rosy
Zak
Samina
Frances
Josey
Quentin
Una

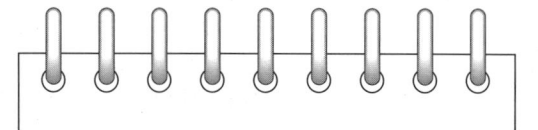

Homework

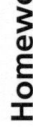

Week 6 — Information texts

'Duck' (from Dorling Kindersley's *See How They Grow* series by Angela Royson)

Introduction

This extract shows the life of a duckling from when it hatches out of the egg to becoming a fully grown duck – a period of six weeks. It is important for children to develop skills in discovering facts from information texts, as well as appreciating the differences between fiction and non-fiction, both in content and layout. Although the text in this explanation is simple, the language is very different from that in a story or poem. The KWL grid and the writing frame (See Day 5) provide opportunities for the children to consider and revise what they have learned, as well as gaining experience with a useful model which can be used with any information text.

Week 6 Objectives

	Word level	Sentence level	Text level
Day 1 Reading	To learn new words from reading Y2 T1 (10)	To read aloud with intonation and expression Y2 T2 (2) To use awareness of grammar to predict new words Y2 T2 (1)	To reinforce and apply word level skills Y2 T2 (1) To understand the distinction between fact and fiction Y2 T3 (13) To identify questions and use text to find answers Y1 T3 (19)
Day 2 Comprehension Vowels	To secure and use the terms *vowel* and *consonant* Y2 T1 (8)		To make sense of what they have read Y2 T3 (2)
Day 3 Spelling: Sight vocabulary, Onset and rime	To recall high-frequency words Y3 T1–3, (3) Spelling by analogy with known words Y3 T1–3 (6)		
Day 4 Word endings Syllables	To use word endings to support reading and spelling Y2 T1 (7) To discriminate syllables in words Y2 T2 (5)		
Day 5 Composition			To make a simple record of information from texts read Y3 T1 (22) To apply phonological and graphic knowledge and sight vocabulary to spell words Y2 T3 (9)
Homework task 1 Word order		To reorder sentences Y1 T3 (4)	
Homework task 2 Comprehension			To make sense of what they read Y2 T3 (2)

Special Needs Literacy
Resources for Group Time

Reading

Before reading
Before looking at the extract on photocopiable pages 47 and 48, begin the KWL grid.
 K = What do I already **k**now?
 W = What do I **w**ant to find out?
 L = What have I **l**earned?

| What do I already know? | What do I want to find out? | What have I learned? |

Each child will need an A4 size version of the grid. To help the children to complete the first column of the KWL grid:
- Ask, 'What do you already know about baby ducks?' Encourage them to write at least one piece of information in the first column.
- Help them to think of a question about ducks. The children should then write their question in the second column.
Give each child a copy of the extract. Ask the children what kind of book they think the extract is from. Is it a story? How do they know?

If necessary, explain to the children that this is a non-fiction or information text. Ask them what the difference is. (Fiction refers to stories and is not necessarily true, but non-fiction is about facts and things which really happen, or things you can do.)

Introducing the extract (see page 4)
Look through the pictures and discuss what is happening. Help the children to find the words *duckling, dabble* and *feathers*. Now read the extract (see pages 47 and 48).

After reading
The children can complete the third column of the KWL grid by writing two facts they have learned from the text. (They may not have found the answers to their earlier questions, in which case they could be encouraged to find other books about ducks, outside the Literacy Hour.)

Comprehension

Quiz (oral answers)
1. What colour is the duckling's down?
A. Yellow.
2. How does a mother duck keep the eggs warm?
A. She sits on them.
3. What does 'hatch' mean?
A. Coming out of the shell.
4. Name three things a duckling can do.
A. See, hear, stand, cheep, walk and swim.
5. Where do ducks find food?
A. In the water.

Quiz (written answers)
1. What do baby ducks have before they grow feathers?
A. Down.
2. What are baby ducks called?
A. Ducklings.
3. Where are duck eggs laid?
A. In a nest.
4. Which word means 'coming out of an egg'?
A. Hatch.
5. What sound do baby ducks make?
A. Cheep.

Vowels
- Can the children remember the five letters which are vowels? (a e i o u).
- Ask the children to look through the extract and to find and colour all the words which begin with vowels.
- The children can make lists of the words they find, for each vowel. For example:

a	e	i	o	u
am	*egg*	*is*	*on*	*untidy*

- Which list is the longest? Which is the shortest?
- Ask the children to write a sentence and to try to include at least three words starting with a vowel. (They do not necessarily have to use the words from the extract.)

Sight vocabulary

Ask the children to find the word *this* in the extract and to learn to spell the word using the Look–Say–Cover–Write–Check method (see page 6) until they can write it from memory. Do the same with *last* and *love*. The children should write the words in their spelling books to take home for further practice.

Help the children to think of a sentence with all three words in it, and to write it down, using a coloured pencil or felt-tipped pen to highlight *this, last* and *love*.

Spelling by analogy

Ask the children to find the word *stand* in the extract and to look carefully at the spelling. What small word can they see in *stand*? (*and*) The children should learn to spell *stand* using the Look–Say–Cover–Write–Check method (see page 6) until they can write it from memory.

Encourage them to think of words that rhyme with stand (*land, band, hand, grand*). Dictate the words for the children to write in their spelling books.

Dictate the following sentences, for the children to write in their spelling books. (Decide whether you want them to have the word list for reference or not.) Remind them about capital letters and full stops, if necessary.

*Can you do a **hand stand**?*
*The **band** is **grand**.*

The children should underline all the *-and* words in their completed sentences with a coloured pencil or felt-tipped pen.

They could make word wheels or flick books with the spelling pattern to take home (see page 6).

Day 3 — Week 6 Information texts

Special Needs Literacy

Word endings

- Direct the children to the 'In the nest' section and ask them to look for a word that has *-ing* at the end (*duckling, growing, beginning*).
- Make sure they can all remember the spelling of the *-ing* ending.
- Ask the children to look through the extract for more *-ing* words. They should make a list of all the words they find.
- Now ask the children to find this sentence:
  *I can **see** and **hear** and **stand** and **walk**.*
- Which word tells you what a duckling can do? (*see, hear, stand, walk*)
- Can the children add *-ing* to each word to make a new word?
- Each child can write a sentence that begins *The duckling is...* and include the four new *-ing* words.

Syllables

Ask the children to find the word *duckling*.
- Clap the syllables in the word (2 claps: *duck/ling*)
- As a group, read aloud the 'In the nest' part of the extract again to find other words that have two syllables (*mother, inside, growing*).
- Is there a word with three syllables? (*beginning*)
- Help the children to count the syllables in these words by clapping as they say the words:

eggs	(1)
pushing	(2)
untidy	(3)
feathers	(2)
together	(3)
sometimes	(2)
feet	(1)

Play 'Guess the word'

Each child in turn chooses a section of the extract and claps the syllables in a word, without saying it aloud. The others have to guess what the word was.

The children choose words of 1, 2 and 3 syllables from the extract. They write each word highlighting each syllable in a different colour.

Day 4 — Week 6 Information texts

Special Needs Literacy
Resources for Group Time

Ducks

Although I already knew that ducks

I have learned some new facts. I learned that

I also learned that

Another fact I learned

However the most interesting thing I learned was

Writing composition:
Ask the children to write about the information they have learned about ducks. Their KWL chart from Day 1 will help them. If they like, they could use pictures as well as words.

Information texts

Word jumble

The words in these sentences about ducklings are mixed up. Can you write each sentence correctly? Look for the capital letter to start each sentence.

1 baby   out   A   of   duck   shell.   the   pushes

_____

_____

2 yellow   The   falls   and   down   grow.   out   feathers

_____

_____

3 love   the   Baby   water.   swim   ducklings   to   in

_____

_____

4 water   food.   in   Ducks   the   dabble   for

_____

_____

5 sit   them   to   Mother   warm.   eggs   ducks   keep   their   on

_____

_____

Information texts

True or false?

Think carefully about the text you have read about ducklings. Then write down whether these sentences are true or false.

1 Mother ducks sit on their eggs.

_____

2 A baby duck is called a duckling.

_____

3 A duckling can't walk.

_____

4 When a duckling is six weeks old it is a duck.

_____

5 Ducklings can swim when they are two weeks old.

_____

6 A duckling's down is white.

_____

Make a mask

1 Take some stiff paper as big as a book. Fold it in half, short sides together.

2 Put some sunglasses along the bottom, halfway across the fold.

3 Draw around the shape. Add an eye, then poke a hole in it with a pencil.

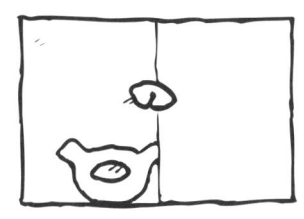

4 Push scissors into the hole. Cut to the edge of the eye, then cut it out. Glue on shiny shapes and sequins.

5 Fold the paper again. Draw around the eye shape onto the paper below.

6 Cut out the other eye shape. Fold the paper and draw a spiky shape.

7 Cut out the shape through both layers. Cut off the bottom corner.

8 Turn the mask over and paint it. Glue on lots of paper shapes.

9 Poke holes in the sides with a pencil. Tie on elastic to fit round your head.

Make a caterpillar

1 Put a book onto a piece of bright paper. Draw around it and cut it out.

2 Fold it in half. Cut along the fold. Sponge different paint on both sides of one piece.

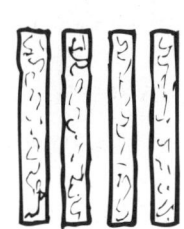

3 Fold the paper in half and in half again. Open it and cut along all the folds.

4 Put some glue at the end of one strip and join it to another one like this.

5 Fold the left strip over and crease it. Fold the other strip down over it.

6 Keep folding one strip over the other one to make a concertina shape.

7 When you get near to the end of the strips, glue on the spare strips, then keep on folding.

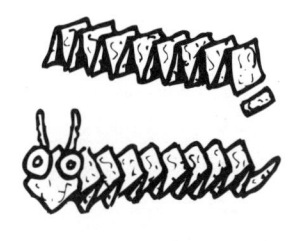

8 When you reach the end glue down the top piece. Trim the ends. Add eyes, feelers and a tail.

9 Tape some thin elastic behind the head and the tail. Tie the caterpillar onto a straw.

A for Alice

A for Alice who climbed a tree,

B for Ben who caught a flea,

C for Carol, playing a trick,

D for Dennis who was awfully sick,

E for Errol, out to play,

F for Fiona, who ran away,

G for Gemma, making bread,

H for Hiroko, under the bed,

I for Ian, flying his kite,

J for Jamal, engaged in a fight.

K for Kate, who came in late,

L for Laura, who thinks she's great,

M for Maria who's always good,

N for Nick, never does what he should,

O for Oliver, in a muddle,

P for Paul who sat down in a puddle,

Q for Queenie, jumping the rope,

R for Rosy who wants to be pope,

S for Shazeia who wins the race,

T for Tracey, making a face,

U for Una, trying to smile,

V for Vijay, dressing in style,

W for Wendy, building a house,

X for Xavier, afraid of a mouse,

Y for Yael who loves to tease,

Z for Zadok who prays on his knees.

June O'Watt

Don't

Why do people say "don't" so much,
Whenever you try something new?
It's more fun doing the don'ting,
So why don't people say "do"?

Don't slurp your spaghetti
Don't kiss the cat
Don't butter your fingers
Don't walk like that
Don't wash your books
Don't bubble your tea
Don't jump on your sister
Don't goggle at me
Don't climb up the curtains
Don't feed the chair
Don't sleep in your wardrobe
Don't cut off your hair
Don't draw on the pillow
Don't change all the clocks
Don't water the phone
Don't hide my socks
Don't cycle upstairs
Don't write on the eggs
Don't chew your pyjamas
Don't paint your legs …

Oh, why do people say "don't" so much,
When ever you try something new?
It's more fun doing the don'ting,
So why don't people say "do"?

Richard Edwards

Duck

In the nest
My mother has laid her eggs in this nest. She sits on them to keep them warm.

Inside each egg a new duckling is growing. This one is me.
I am just beginning to hatch.

Just hatched
I have chipped away my shell and now I am pushing myself out.

At last I am out of my egg. I can see and hear and stand and walk. I can cheep too. Where is my mother?

In the water
I am two weeks old and I love to swim in the water.

I dabble in the water for things to eat.
I shake the water off my feathers.

New feathers
I am three weeks old.
My yellow down is falling out and new white feathers are beginning to grow.

I stay close to the other ducklings.
Our mother watches out for danger.

Sometimes we huddle together. Our untidy feathers help to keep us warm.

Nearly grown up
I am six weeks old and nearly grown up.

All my feathers are white and my wings are bigger and stronger.

See how much I have grown. This bowl is small now, but it seemed big when I first jumped into it.